MW01610798

THIS BOOK BELONGS TO:

_____

_____

IF FOUND PLEASE CONTACT

NAME: _____

EMAIL: _____

TELEPHONE: _____

ADDRESS: _____

THANK YOU

MY EMAIL ADDRESSES

EMAIL:

PASSWORD:

NOTES:

EMAIL:

PASSWORD:

NOTES:

EMAIL:

PASSWORD:

NOTES:

EMAIL:

PASSWORD:

NOTES:

EMAIL:

PASSWORD:

NOTES:

MY EMAIL ADDRESSES

EMAIL:

PASSWORD:

NOTES:

EMAIL:

PASSWORD:

NOTES:

EMAIL:

PASSWORD:

NOTES:

EMAIL:

PASSWORD:

NOTES:

EMAIL:

PASSWORD:

NOTES:

MY EMAIL ADDRESSES

EMAIL:

PASSWORD:

NOTES:

EMAIL:

PASSWORD:

NOTES:

EMAIL:

PASSWORD:

NOTES:

EMAIL:

PASSWORD:

NOTES:

EMAIL:

PASSWORD:

NOTES:

WEBSITE:

USERNAME:

PASSWORD:

NOTES:

WEBSITE:

USERNAME:

PASSWORD:

NOTES:

WEBSITE:

USERNAME:

PASSWORD:

NOTES:

WEBSITE:

USERNAME:

PASSWORD:

NOTES:

A

🌐 WEBSITE:

👤 USERNAME:

🔒 PASSWORD:

📋 NOTES:

🌐 WEBSITE:

👤 USERNAME:

🔒 PASSWORD:

📋 NOTES:

🌐 WEBSITE:

👤 USERNAME:

🔒 PASSWORD:

📋 NOTES:

🌐 WEBSITE:

👤 USERNAME:

🔒 PASSWORD:

📋 NOTES:

WEBSITE: _____

USERNAME: _____

PASSWORD: _____

NOTES: _____
_____

WEBSITE: _____

USERNAME: _____

PASSWORD: _____

NOTES: _____
_____

WEBSITE: _____

USERNAME: _____

PASSWORD: _____

NOTES: _____
_____

WEBSITE: _____

USERNAME: _____

PASSWORD: _____

NOTES: _____
_____

A

🌐 WEBSITE:

👤 USERNAME:

🔒 PASSWORD:

📋 NOTES:

🌐 WEBSITE:

👤 USERNAME:

🔒 PASSWORD:

📋 NOTES:

🌐 WEBSITE:

👤 USERNAME:

🔒 PASSWORD:

📋 NOTES:

🌐 WEBSITE:

👤 USERNAME:

🔒 PASSWORD:

📋 NOTES:

WEBSITE:

USERNAME:

PASSWORD:

NOTES:

WEBSITE:

USERNAME:

PASSWORD:

NOTES:

WEBSITE:

USERNAME:

PASSWORD:

NOTES:

WEBSITE:

USERNAME:

PASSWORD:

NOTES:

B

🌐 WEBSITE:

👤 USERNAME:

🔒 PASSWORD:

📋 NOTES:

🌐 WEBSITE:

👤 USERNAME:

🔒 PASSWORD:

📋 NOTES:

🌐 WEBSITE:

👤 USERNAME:

🔒 PASSWORD:

📋 NOTES:

🌐 WEBSITE:

👤 USERNAME:

🔒 PASSWORD:

📋 NOTES:

WEBSITE:

USERNAME:

PASSWORD:

NOTES:

WEBSITE:

USERNAME:

PASSWORD:

NOTES:

WEBSITE:

USERNAME:

PASSWORD:

NOTES:

WEBSITE:

USERNAME:

PASSWORD:

NOTES:

⊕ WEBSITE: _____

⊗ USERNAME: _____

🔒 PASSWORD: _____

📋 NOTES: _____

_____

⊕ WEBSITE: _____

⊗ USERNAME: _____

🔒 PASSWORD: _____

📋 NOTES: _____

_____

⊕ WEBSITE: _____

⊗ USERNAME: _____

🔒 PASSWORD: _____

📋 NOTES: _____

_____

⊕ WEBSITE: _____

⊗ USERNAME: _____

🔒 PASSWORD: _____

📋 NOTES: _____

_____

WEBSITE:

USERNAME:

PASSWORD:

NOTES:

WEBSITE:

USERNAME:

PASSWORD:

NOTES:

WEBSITE:

USERNAME:

PASSWORD:

NOTES:

WEBSITE:

USERNAME:

PASSWORD:

NOTES:

🌐 WEBSITE:

👤 USERNAME:

🔒 PASSWORD:

📋 NOTES:

🌐 WEBSITE:

👤 USERNAME:

🔒 PASSWORD:

📋 NOTES:

🌐 WEBSITE:

👤 USERNAME:

🔒 PASSWORD:

📋 NOTES:

🌐 WEBSITE:

👤 USERNAME:

🔒 PASSWORD:

📋 NOTES:

🌐 WEBSITE: _____

👤 USERNAME: _____

🔒 PASSWORD: _____

📋 NOTES: _____

_____

🌐 WEBSITE: _____

👤 USERNAME: _____

🔒 PASSWORD: _____

📋 NOTES: _____

_____

🌐 WEBSITE: _____

👤 USERNAME: _____

🔒 PASSWORD: _____

📋 NOTES: _____

_____

🌐 WEBSITE: _____

👤 USERNAME: _____

🔒 PASSWORD: _____

📋 NOTES: _____

_____

C

🌐 WEBSITE: _____

👤 USERNAME: _____

🔒 PASSWORD: _____

📋 NOTES: _____

_____

🌐 WEBSITE: _____

👤 USERNAME: _____

🔒 PASSWORD: _____

📋 NOTES: _____

_____

🌐 WEBSITE: _____

👤 USERNAME: _____

🔒 PASSWORD: _____

📋 NOTES: _____

_____

🌐 WEBSITE: _____

👤 USERNAME: _____

🔒 PASSWORD: _____

📋 NOTES: _____

_____

WEBSITE:

USERNAME:

PASSWORD:

NOTES:

WEBSITE:

USERNAME:

PASSWORD:

NOTES:

WEBSITE:

USERNAME:

PASSWORD:

NOTES:

WEBSITE:

USERNAME:

PASSWORD:

NOTES:

D

⊕ WEBSITE:

☻ USERNAME:

🔒 PASSWORD:

📋 NOTES:

⊕ WEBSITE:

☻ USERNAME:

🔒 PASSWORD:

📋 NOTES:

⊕ WEBSITE:

☻ USERNAME:

🔒 PASSWORD:

📋 NOTES:

⊕ WEBSITE:

☻ USERNAME:

🔒 PASSWORD:

📋 NOTES:

⊕ WEBSITE: _____

⊘ USERNAME: _____

🔒 PASSWORD: _____

📋 NOTES: _____

_____

_____

⊕ WEBSITE: _____

⊘ USERNAME: _____

🔒 PASSWORD: _____

📋 NOTES: _____

_____

_____

⊕ WEBSITE: _____

⊘ USERNAME: _____

🔒 PASSWORD: _____

📋 NOTES: _____

_____

_____

⊕ WEBSITE: _____

⊘ USERNAME: _____

🔒 PASSWORD: _____

📋 NOTES: _____

_____

D

🌐 WEBSITE:

👤 USERNAME:

🔒 PASSWORD:

📋 NOTES:

🌐 WEBSITE:

👤 USERNAME:

🔒 PASSWORD:

📋 NOTES:

🌐 WEBSITE:

👤 USERNAME:

🔒 PASSWORD:

📋 NOTES:

🌐 WEBSITE:

👤 USERNAME:

🔒 PASSWORD:

📋 NOTES:

WEBSITE:

USERNAME:

PASSWORD:

NOTES:

WEBSITE:

USERNAME:

PASSWORD:

NOTES:

WEBSITE:

USERNAME:

PASSWORD:

NOTES:

WEBSITE:

USERNAME:

PASSWORD:

NOTES:

WEBSITE:

USERNAME:

PASSWORD:

NOTES:

WEBSITE:

USERNAME:

PASSWORD:

NOTES:

WEBSITE:

USERNAME:

PASSWORD:

NOTES:

WEBSITE:

USERNAME:

PASSWORD:

NOTES:

WEBSITE:

USERNAME:

PASSWORD:

NOTES:

WEBSITE:

USERNAME:

PASSWORD:

NOTES:

WEBSITE:

USERNAME:

PASSWORD:

NOTES:

WEBSITE:

USERNAME:

PASSWORD:

NOTES:

E

WEBSITE:

USERNAME:

PASSWORD:

NOTES:

WEBSITE:

USERNAME:

PASSWORD:

NOTES:

WEBSITE:

USERNAME:

PASSWORD:

NOTES:

WEBSITE:

USERNAME:

PASSWORD:

NOTES:

WEBSITE:

USERNAME:

PASSWORD:

NOTES:

WEBSITE:

USERNAME:

PASSWORD:

NOTES:

WEBSITE:

USERNAME:

PASSWORD:

NOTES:

WEBSITE:

USERNAME:

PASSWORD:

NOTES:

🌐 WEBSITE:

👤 USERNAME:

🔒 PASSWORD:

📋 NOTES:

🌐 WEBSITE:

👤 USERNAME:

🔒 PASSWORD:

📋 NOTES:

🌐 WEBSITE:

👤 USERNAME:

🔒 PASSWORD:

📋 NOTES:

🌐 WEBSITE:

👤 USERNAME:

🔒 PASSWORD:

📋 NOTES:

WEBSITE:

USERNAME:

PASSWORD:

NOTES:

WEBSITE:

USERNAME:

PASSWORD:

NOTES:

WEBSITE:

USERNAME:

PASSWORD:

NOTES:

WEBSITE:

USERNAME:

PASSWORD:

NOTES:

F

⊕ WEBSITE:

⊙ USERNAME:

🔒 PASSWORD:

📋 NOTES:

⊕ WEBSITE:

⊙ USERNAME:

🔒 PASSWORD:

📋 NOTES:

⊕ WEBSITE:

⊙ USERNAME:

🔒 PASSWORD:

📋 NOTES:

⊕ WEBSITE:

⊙ USERNAME:

🔒 PASSWORD:

📋 NOTES:

WEBSITE:

USERNAME:

PASSWORD:

NOTES:

WEBSITE:

USERNAME:

PASSWORD:

NOTES:

WEBSITE:

USERNAME:

PASSWORD:

NOTES:

WEBSITE:

USERNAME:

PASSWORD:

NOTES:

G

⊕ WEBSITE: _____

👤 USERNAME: _____

🔒 PASSWORD: _____

📋 NOTES: _____

_____

⊕ WEBSITE: _____

👤 USERNAME: _____

🔒 PASSWORD: _____

📋 NOTES: _____

_____

⊕ WEBSITE: _____

👤 USERNAME: _____

🔒 PASSWORD: _____

📋 NOTES: _____

_____

⊕ WEBSITE: _____

👤 USERNAME: _____

🔒 PASSWORD: _____

📋 NOTES: _____

_____

WEBSITE:

USERNAME:

PASSWORD:

NOTES:

WEBSITE:

USERNAME:

PASSWORD:

NOTES:

WEBSITE:

USERNAME:

PASSWORD:

NOTES:

WEBSITE:

USERNAME:

PASSWORD:

NOTES:

WEBSITE:

USERNAME:

PASSWORD:

NOTES:

WEBSITE:

USERNAME:

PASSWORD:

NOTES:

WEBSITE:

USERNAME:

PASSWORD:

NOTES:

WEBSITE:

USERNAME:

PASSWORD:

NOTES:

WEBSITE:

USERNAME:

PASSWORD:

NOTES:

WEBSITE:

USERNAME:

PASSWORD:

NOTES:

WEBSITE:

USERNAME:

PASSWORD:

NOTES:

WEBSITE:

USERNAME:

PASSWORD:

NOTES:

WEBSITE:

USERNAME:

PASSWORD:

NOTES:

WEBSITE:

USERNAME:

PASSWORD:

NOTES:

WEBSITE:

USERNAME:

PASSWORD:

NOTES:

WEBSITE:

USERNAME:

PASSWORD:

NOTES:

WEBSITE:

USERNAME:

PASSWORD:

NOTES:

WEBSITE:

USERNAME:

PASSWORD:

NOTES:

WEBSITE:

USERNAME:

PASSWORD:

NOTES:

WEBSITE:

USERNAME:

PASSWORD:

NOTES:

🌐 WEBSITE: _____

👤 USERNAME: _____

🔒 PASSWORD: _____

📋 NOTES: _____

_____

🌐 WEBSITE: _____

👤 USERNAME: _____

🔒 PASSWORD: _____

📋 NOTES: _____

_____

🌐 WEBSITE: _____

👤 USERNAME: _____

🔒 PASSWORD: _____

📋 NOTES: _____

_____

🌐 WEBSITE: _____

👤 USERNAME: _____

🔒 PASSWORD: _____

📋 NOTES: _____

_____

WEBSITE:

USERNAME:

PASSWORD:

NOTES:

WEBSITE:

USERNAME:

PASSWORD:

NOTES:

WEBSITE:

USERNAME:

PASSWORD:

NOTES:

WEBSITE:

USERNAME:

PASSWORD:

NOTES:

I

🌐 WEBSITE:

👤 USERNAME:

🔒 PASSWORD:

📋 NOTES:

🌐 WEBSITE:

👤 USERNAME:

🔒 PASSWORD:

📋 NOTES:

🌐 WEBSITE:

👤 USERNAME:

🔒 PASSWORD:

📋 NOTES:

🌐 WEBSITE:

👤 USERNAME:

🔒 PASSWORD:

📋 NOTES:

WEBSITE:

USERNAME:

PASSWORD:

NOTES:

WEBSITE:

USERNAME:

PASSWORD:

NOTES:

WEBSITE:

USERNAME:

PASSWORD:

NOTES:

WEBSITE:

USERNAME:

PASSWORD:

NOTES:

🌐 WEBSITE:

👤 USERNAME:

🔒 PASSWORD:

📝 NOTES:

🌐 WEBSITE:

👤 USERNAME:

🔒 PASSWORD:

📝 NOTES:

🌐 WEBSITE:

👤 USERNAME:

🔒 PASSWORD:

📝 NOTES:

🌐 WEBSITE:

👤 USERNAME:

🔒 PASSWORD:

📝 NOTES:

WEBSITE:

USERNAME:

PASSWORD:

NOTES:

WEBSITE:

USERNAME:

PASSWORD:

NOTES:

WEBSITE:

USERNAME:

PASSWORD:

NOTES:

WEBSITE:

USERNAME:

PASSWORD:

NOTES:

J

🌐 WEBSITE: _____

👤 USERNAME: _____

🔒 PASSWORD: _____

📋 NOTES: _____

_____

🌐 WEBSITE: _____

👤 USERNAME: _____

🔒 PASSWORD: _____

📋 NOTES: _____

_____

🌐 WEBSITE: _____

👤 USERNAME: _____

🔒 PASSWORD: _____

📋 NOTES: _____

_____

🌐 WEBSITE: _____

👤 USERNAME: _____

🔒 PASSWORD: _____

📋 NOTES: _____

_____

⊕ WEBSITE: _____

⊙ USERNAME: _____

🔒 PASSWORD: _____

📋 NOTES: _____

_____

_____

⊕ WEBSITE: _____

⊙ USERNAME: _____

🔒 PASSWORD: _____

📋 NOTES: _____

_____

_____

⊕ WEBSITE: _____

⊙ USERNAME: _____

🔒 PASSWORD: _____

📋 NOTES: _____

_____

_____

⊕ WEBSITE: _____

⊙ USERNAME: _____

🔒 PASSWORD: _____

📋 NOTES: _____

_____

J

🌐 WEBSITE:

👤 USERNAME:

🔒 PASSWORD:

📋 NOTES:

🌐 WEBSITE:

👤 USERNAME:

🔒 PASSWORD:

📋 NOTES:

🌐 WEBSITE:

👤 USERNAME:

🔒 PASSWORD:

📋 NOTES:

🌐 WEBSITE:

👤 USERNAME:

🔒 PASSWORD:

📋 NOTES:

⊕ WEBSITE:

⊘ USERNAME:

🔒 PASSWORD:

📋 NOTES:

⊕ WEBSITE:

⊘ USERNAME:

🔒 PASSWORD:

📋 NOTES:

⊕ WEBSITE:

⊘ USERNAME:

🔒 PASSWORD:

📋 NOTES:

⊕ WEBSITE:

⊘ USERNAME:

🔒 PASSWORD:

📋 NOTES:

🌐WEBSITE:

👤USERNAME:

🔒 PASSWORD:

📋NOTES:

🌐WEBSITE:

👤USERNAME:

🔒 PASSWORD:

📋NOTES:

🌐WEBSITE:

👤USERNAME:

🔒 PASSWORD:

📋NOTES:

🌐WEBSITE:

👤USERNAME:

🔒 PASSWORD:

📋NOTES:

WEBSITE:

USERNAME:

PASSWORD:

NOTES:

WEBSITE:

USERNAME:

PASSWORD:

NOTES:

WEBSITE:

USERNAME:

PASSWORD:

NOTES:

WEBSITE:

USERNAME:

PASSWORD:

NOTES:

K

🌐 WEBSITE: _____

👤 USERNAME: _____

🔒 PASSWORD: _____

📋 NOTES: _____

_____

🌐 WEBSITE: _____

👤 USERNAME: _____

🔒 PASSWORD: _____

📋 NOTES: _____

_____

🌐 WEBSITE: _____

👤 USERNAME: _____

🔒 PASSWORD: _____

📋 NOTES: _____

_____

🌐 WEBSITE: _____

👤 USERNAME: _____

🔒 PASSWORD: _____

📋 NOTES: _____

_____

WEBSITE:

USERNAME:

PASSWORD:

NOTES:

WEBSITE:

USERNAME:

PASSWORD:

NOTES:

WEBSITE:

USERNAME:

PASSWORD:

NOTES:

WEBSITE:

USERNAME:

PASSWORD:

NOTES:

🌐 WEBSITE: _____

👤 USERNAME: _____

🔒 PASSWORD: _____

📋 NOTES: _____

_____

🌐 WEBSITE: _____

👤 USERNAME: _____

🔒 PASSWORD: _____

📋 NOTES: _____

_____

🌐 WEBSITE: _____

👤 USERNAME: _____

🔒 PASSWORD: _____

📋 NOTES: _____

_____

🌐 WEBSITE: _____

👤 USERNAME: _____

🔒 PASSWORD: _____

📋 NOTES: _____

_____

WEBSITE:

USERNAME:

PASSWORD:

NOTES:

WEBSITE:

USERNAME:

PASSWORD:

NOTES:

WEBSITE:

USERNAME:

PASSWORD:

NOTES:

WEBSITE:

USERNAME:

PASSWORD:

NOTES:

🌐 WEBSITE:

👤 USERNAME:

🔒 PASSWORD:

📋 NOTES:

🌐 WEBSITE:

👤 USERNAME:

🔒 PASSWORD:

📋 NOTES:

🌐 WEBSITE:

👤 USERNAME:

🔒 PASSWORD:

📋 NOTES:

🌐 WEBSITE:

👤 USERNAME:

🔒 PASSWORD:

📋 NOTES:

WEBSITE: _____

USERNAME: _____

PASSWORD: _____

NOTES: _____

_____

WEBSITE: _____

USERNAME: _____

PASSWORD: _____

NOTES: _____

_____

WEBSITE: _____

USERNAME: _____

PASSWORD: _____

NOTES: _____

_____

WEBSITE: _____

USERNAME: _____

PASSWORD: _____

NOTES: _____

_____

M

🌐 WEBSITE:

👤 USERNAME:

🔒 PASSWORD:

📋 NOTES:

🌐 WEBSITE:

👤 USERNAME:

🔒 PASSWORD:

📋 NOTES:

🌐 WEBSITE:

👤 USERNAME:

🔒 PASSWORD:

📋 NOTES:

🌐 WEBSITE:

👤 USERNAME:

🔒 PASSWORD:

📋 NOTES:

WEBSITE:

USERNAME:

PASSWORD:

NOTES:

WEBSITE:

USERNAME:

PASSWORD:

NOTES:

WEBSITE:

USERNAME:

PASSWORD:

NOTES:

WEBSITE:

USERNAME:

PASSWORD:

NOTES:

M

🌐 WEBSITE:

👤 USERNAME:

🔒 PASSWORD:

📝 NOTES:

🌐 WEBSITE:

👤 USERNAME:

🔒 PASSWORD:

📝 NOTES:

🌐 WEBSITE:

👤 USERNAME:

🔒 PASSWORD:

📝 NOTES:

🌐 WEBSITE:

👤 USERNAME:

🔒 PASSWORD:

📝 NOTES:

WEBSITE: _____

USERNAME: _____

PASSWORD: _____

NOTES: _____

_____

WEBSITE: _____

USERNAME: _____

PASSWORD: _____

NOTES: _____

_____

WEBSITE: _____

USERNAME: _____

PASSWORD: _____

NOTES: _____

_____

WEBSITE: _____

USERNAME: _____

PASSWORD: _____

NOTES: _____

_____

⊕ WEBSITE:

⊗ USERNAME:

🔒 PASSWORD:

📋 NOTES:

⊕ WEBSITE:

⊗ USERNAME:

🔒 PASSWORD:

📋 NOTES:

⊕ WEBSITE:

⊗ USERNAME:

🔒 PASSWORD:

📋 NOTES:

⊕ WEBSITE:

⊗ USERNAME:

🔒 PASSWORD:

📋 NOTES:

WEBSITE:

USERNAME:

PASSWORD:

NOTES:

WEBSITE:

USERNAME:

PASSWORD:

NOTES:

WEBSITE:

USERNAME:

PASSWORD:

NOTES:

WEBSITE:

USERNAME:

PASSWORD:

NOTES:

WEBSITE:

USERNAME:

PASSWORD:

NOTES:

WEBSITE:

USERNAME:

PASSWORD:

NOTES:

WEBSITE:

USERNAME:

PASSWORD:

NOTES:

WEBSITE:

USERNAME:

PASSWORD:

NOTES:

WEBSITE:

USERNAME:

PASSWORD:

NOTES:

WEBSITE:

USERNAME:

PASSWORD:

NOTES:

WEBSITE:

USERNAME:

PASSWORD:

NOTES:

WEBSITE:

USERNAME:

PASSWORD:

NOTES:

WEBSITE: _____

 USERNAME: _____

 PASSWORD: _____

 NOTES: _____

_____

_____

 WEBSITE: _____

 USERNAME: _____

 PASSWORD: _____

 NOTES: _____

_____

_____

 WEBSITE: _____

 USERNAME: _____

 PASSWORD: _____

 NOTES: _____

_____

_____

 WEBSITE: _____

 USERNAME: _____

 PASSWORD: _____

 NOTES: _____

_____

⊕ WEBSITE:

⊖ USERNAME:

🔒 PASSWORD:

📝 NOTES:

⊕ WEBSITE:

⊖ USERNAME:

🔒 PASSWORD:

📝 NOTES:

⊕ WEBSITE:

⊖ USERNAME:

🔒 PASSWORD:

📝 NOTES:

⊕ WEBSITE:

⊖ USERNAME:

🔒 PASSWORD:

📝 NOTES:

⊕ WEBSITE:

⊘ USERNAME:

🔒 PASSWORD:

📋 NOTES:

⊕ WEBSITE:

⊘ USERNAME:

🔒 PASSWORD:

📋 NOTES:

⊕ WEBSITE:

⊘ USERNAME:

🔒 PASSWORD:

📋 NOTES:

⊕ WEBSITE:

⊘ USERNAME:

🔒 PASSWORD:

📋 NOTES:

WEBSITE:

USERNAME:

PASSWORD:

NOTES:

WEBSITE:

USERNAME:

PASSWORD:

NOTES:

WEBSITE:

USERNAME:

PASSWORD:

NOTES:

WEBSITE:

USERNAME:

PASSWORD:

NOTES:

p

⊕ WEBSITE:

⊖ USERNAME:

🔒 PASSWORD:

📋 NOTES:

⊕ WEBSITE:

⊖ USERNAME:

🔒 PASSWORD:

📋 NOTES:

⊕ WEBSITE:

⊖ USERNAME:

🔒 PASSWORD:

📋 NOTES:

⊕ WEBSITE:

⊖ USERNAME:

🔒 PASSWORD:

📋 NOTES:

WEBSITE:

USERNAME:

PASSWORD:

NOTES:

WEBSITE:

USERNAME:

PASSWORD:

NOTES:

WEBSITE:

USERNAME:

PASSWORD:

NOTES:

WEBSITE:

USERNAME:

PASSWORD:

NOTES:

p

⊕ WEBSITE:

⊙ USERNAME:

🔒 PASSWORD:

📋 NOTES:

⊕ WEBSITE:

⊙ USERNAME:

🔒 PASSWORD:

📋 NOTES:

⊕ WEBSITE:

⊙ USERNAME:

🔒 PASSWORD:

📋 NOTES:

⊕ WEBSITE:

⊙ USERNAME:

🔒 PASSWORD:

📋 NOTES:

WEBSITE:

USERNAME:

PASSWORD:

NOTES:

WEBSITE:

USERNAME:

PASSWORD:

NOTES:

WEBSITE:

USERNAME:

PASSWORD:

NOTES:

WEBSITE:

USERNAME:

PASSWORD:

NOTES:

⊕ WEBSITE:

⊗ USERNAME:

🔒 PASSWORD:

📋 NOTES:

⊕ WEBSITE:

⊗ USERNAME:

🔒 PASSWORD:

📋 NOTES:

⊕ WEBSITE:

⊗ USERNAME:

🔒 PASSWORD:

📋 NOTES:

⊕ WEBSITE:

⊗ USERNAME:

🔒 PASSWORD:

📋 NOTES:

WEBSITE:

USERNAME:

PASSWORD:

NOTES:

WEBSITE:

USERNAME:

PASSWORD:

NOTES:

WEBSITE:

USERNAME:

PASSWORD:

NOTES:

WEBSITE:

USERNAME:

PASSWORD:

NOTES:

Q

🌐 WEBSITE: _____

👤 USERNAME: _____

🔒 PASSWORD: _____

📋 NOTES: _____

_____

🌐 WEBSITE: _____

👤 USERNAME: _____

🔒 PASSWORD: _____

📋 NOTES: _____

_____

🌐 WEBSITE: _____

👤 USERNAME: _____

🔒 PASSWORD: _____

📋 NOTES: _____

_____

🌐 WEBSITE: _____

👤 USERNAME: _____

🔒 PASSWORD: _____

📋 NOTES: _____

_____

WEBSITE:

USERNAME:

PASSWORD:

NOTES:

WEBSITE:

USERNAME:

PASSWORD:

NOTES:

WEBSITE:

USERNAME:

PASSWORD:

NOTES:

WEBSITE:

USERNAME:

PASSWORD:

NOTES:

R

🌐 WEBSITE: _____

👤 USERNAME: _____

🔒 PASSWORD: _____

📋 NOTES: _____

_____

🌐 WEBSITE: _____

👤 USERNAME: _____

🔒 PASSWORD: _____

📋 NOTES: _____

_____

🌐 WEBSITE: _____

👤 USERNAME: _____

🔒 PASSWORD: _____

📋 NOTES: _____

_____

🌐 WEBSITE: _____

👤 USERNAME: _____

🔒 PASSWORD: _____

📋 NOTES: _____

_____

WEBSITE:

USERNAME:

PASSWORD:

NOTES:

WEBSITE:

USERNAME:

PASSWORD:

NOTES:

WEBSITE:

USERNAME:

PASSWORD:

NOTES:

WEBSITE:

USERNAME:

PASSWORD:

NOTES:

WEBSITE:

USERNAME:

PASSWORD:

NOTES:

WEBSITE:

USERNAME:

PASSWORD:

NOTES:

WEBSITE:

USERNAME:

PASSWORD:

NOTES:

WEBSITE:

USERNAME:

PASSWORD:

NOTES:

WEBSITE:

USERNAME:

PASSWORD:

NOTES:

WEBSITE:

USERNAME:

PASSWORD:

NOTES:

WEBSITE:

USERNAME:

PASSWORD:

NOTES:

WEBSITE:

USERNAME:

PASSWORD:

NOTES:

WEBSITE:

USERNAME:

PASSWORD:

NOTES:

WEBSITE:

USERNAME:

PASSWORD:

NOTES:

WEBSITE:

USERNAME:

PASSWORD:

NOTES:

WEBSITE:

USERNAME:

PASSWORD:

NOTES:

WEBSITE:

USERNAME:

PASSWORD:

NOTES:

WEBSITE:

USERNAME:

PASSWORD:

NOTES:

WEBSITE:

USERNAME:

PASSWORD:

NOTES:

WEBSITE:

USERNAME:

PASSWORD:

NOTES:

WEBSITE: _____

USERNAME: _____

PASSWORD: _____

NOTES: _____

_____

WEBSITE: _____

USERNAME: _____

PASSWORD: _____

NOTES: _____

_____

WEBSITE: _____

USERNAME: _____

PASSWORD: _____

NOTES: _____

_____

WEBSITE: _____

USERNAME: _____

PASSWORD: _____

NOTES: _____

_____

WEBSITE: _____

USERNAME: _____

PASSWORD: _____

NOTES: _____

_____

_____

WEBSITE: _____

USERNAME: _____

PASSWORD: _____

NOTES: _____

_____

_____

WEBSITE: _____

USERNAME: _____

PASSWORD: _____

NOTES: _____

_____

_____

WEBSITE: _____

USERNAME: _____

PASSWORD: _____

NOTES: _____

_____

WEBSITE:

USERNAME:

PASSWORD:

NOTES:

WEBSITE:

USERNAME:

PASSWORD:

NOTES:

WEBSITE:

USERNAME:

PASSWORD:

NOTES:

WEBSITE:

USERNAME:

PASSWORD:

NOTES:

🌐 WEBSITE:

👤 USERNAME:

🔒 PASSWORD:

📋 NOTES:

🌐 WEBSITE:

👤 USERNAME:

🔒 PASSWORD:

📋 NOTES:

🌐 WEBSITE:

👤 USERNAME:

🔒 PASSWORD:

📋 NOTES:

🌐 WEBSITE:

👤 USERNAME:

🔒 PASSWORD:

📋 NOTES:

T

🌐 WEBSITE:

👤 USERNAME:

🔒 PASSWORD:

📋 NOTES:

🌐 WEBSITE:

👤 USERNAME:

🔒 PASSWORD:

📋 NOTES:

🌐 WEBSITE:

👤 USERNAME:

🔒 PASSWORD:

📋 NOTES:

🌐 WEBSITE:

👤 USERNAME:

🔒 PASSWORD:

📋 NOTES:

WEBSITE:

USERNAME:

PASSWORD:

NOTES:

WEBSITE:

USERNAME:

PASSWORD:

NOTES:

WEBSITE:

USERNAME:

PASSWORD:

NOTES:

WEBSITE:

USERNAME:

PASSWORD:

NOTES:

U

⊕ WEBSITE:

⊗ USERNAME:

🔒 PASSWORD:

📋 NOTES:

⊕ WEBSITE:

⊗ USERNAME:

🔒 PASSWORD:

📋 NOTES:

⊕ WEBSITE:

⊗ USERNAME:

🔒 PASSWORD:

📋 NOTES:

⊕ WEBSITE:

⊗ USERNAME:

🔒 PASSWORD:

📋 NOTES:

WEBSITE:

USERNAME:

PASSWORD:

NOTES:

WEBSITE:

USERNAME:

PASSWORD:

NOTES:

WEBSITE:

USERNAME:

PASSWORD:

NOTES:

WEBSITE:

USERNAME:

PASSWORD:

NOTES:

U

⊕ WEBSITE: _____

⊗ USERNAME: _____

🔒 PASSWORD: _____

📋 NOTES: _____

_____

_____

⊕ WEBSITE: _____

⊗ USERNAME: _____

🔒 PASSWORD: _____

📋 NOTES: _____

_____

_____

⊕ WEBSITE: _____

⊗ USERNAME: _____

🔒 PASSWORD: _____

📋 NOTES: _____

_____

_____

⊕ WEBSITE: _____

⊗ USERNAME: _____

🔒 PASSWORD: _____

📋 NOTES: _____

_____

WEBSITE:

USERNAME:

PASSWORD:

NOTES:

WEBSITE:

USERNAME:

PASSWORD:

NOTES:

WEBSITE:

USERNAME:

PASSWORD:

NOTES:

WEBSITE:

USERNAME:

PASSWORD:

NOTES:

WEBSITE:

USERNAME:

PASSWORD:

NOTES:

WEBSITE:

USERNAME:

PASSWORD:

NOTES:

WEBSITE:

USERNAME:

PASSWORD:

NOTES:

WEBSITE:

USERNAME:

PASSWORD:

NOTES:

WEBSITE:

USERNAME:

PASSWORD:

NOTES:

WEBSITE:

USERNAME:

PASSWORD:

NOTES:

WEBSITE:

USERNAME:

PASSWORD:

NOTES:

WEBSITE:

USERNAME:

PASSWORD:

NOTES:

WEBSITE:

USERNAME:

PASSWORD:

NOTES:

WEBSITE:

USERNAME:

PASSWORD:

NOTES:

WEBSITE:

USERNAME:

PASSWORD:

NOTES:

WEBSITE:

USERNAME:

PASSWORD:

NOTES:

⊕ WEBSITE:

⊗ USERNAME:

🔒 PASSWORD:

📝 NOTES:

⊕ WEBSITE:

⊗ USERNAME:

🔒 PASSWORD:

📝 NOTES:

⊕ WEBSITE:

⊗ USERNAME:

🔒 PASSWORD:

📝 NOTES:

⊕ WEBSITE:

⊗ USERNAME:

🔒 PASSWORD:

📝 NOTES:

WEBSITE:

USERNAME:

PASSWORD:

NOTES:

WEBSITE:

USERNAME:

PASSWORD:

NOTES:

WEBSITE:

USERNAME:

PASSWORD:

NOTES:

WEBSITE:

USERNAME:

PASSWORD:

NOTES:

WEBSITE:

USERNAME:

PASSWORD:

NOTES:

WEBSITE:

USERNAME:

PASSWORD:

NOTES:

WEBSITE:

USERNAME:

PASSWORD:

NOTES:

WEBSITE:

USERNAME:

PASSWORD:

NOTES:

WEBSITE: _____

USERNAME: _____

PASSWORD: _____

NOTES: _____
_____

WEBSITE: _____

USERNAME: _____

PASSWORD: _____

NOTES: _____
_____

WEBSITE: _____

USERNAME: _____

PASSWORD: _____

NOTES: _____
_____

WEBSITE: _____

USERNAME: _____

PASSWORD: _____

NOTES: _____
_____

🌐 WEBSITE:

👤 USERNAME:

🔒 PASSWORD:

📋 NOTES:

🌐 WEBSITE:

👤 USERNAME:

🔒 PASSWORD:

📋 NOTES:

🌐 WEBSITE:

👤 USERNAME:

🔒 PASSWORD:

📋 NOTES:

🌐 WEBSITE:

👤 USERNAME:

🔒 PASSWORD:

📋 NOTES:

WEBSITE:

USERNAME:

PASSWORD:

NOTES:

WEBSITE:

USERNAME:

PASSWORD:

NOTES:

WEBSITE:

USERNAME:

PASSWORD:

NOTES:

WEBSITE:

USERNAME:

PASSWORD:

NOTES:

WEBSITE:

USERNAME:

PASSWORD:

NOTES:

WEBSITE:

USERNAME:

PASSWORD:

NOTES:

WEBSITE:

USERNAME:

PASSWORD:

NOTES:

WEBSITE:

USERNAME:

PASSWORD:

NOTES:

⊕ WEBSITE:

⊗ USERNAME:

🔒 PASSWORD:

📋 NOTES:

⊕ WEBSITE:

⊗ USERNAME:

🔒 PASSWORD:

📋 NOTES:

⊕ WEBSITE:

⊗ USERNAME:

🔒 PASSWORD:

📋 NOTES:

⊕ WEBSITE:

⊗ USERNAME:

🔒 PASSWORD:

📋 NOTES:

⊕WEBSITE:

⊛USERNAME:

🔒PASSWORD:

📋NOTES:

⊕WEBSITE:

⊛USERNAME:

🔒PASSWORD:

📋NOTES:

⊕WEBSITE:

⊛USERNAME:

🔒PASSWORD:

📋NOTES:

⊕WEBSITE:

⊛USERNAME:

🔒PASSWORD:

📋NOTES:

WEBSITE:

USERNAME:

PASSWORD:

NOTES:

WEBSITE:

USERNAME:

PASSWORD:

NOTES:

WEBSITE:

USERNAME:

PASSWORD:

NOTES:

WEBSITE:

USERNAME:

PASSWORD:

NOTES:

WEBSITE:

USERNAME:

PASSWORD:

NOTES:

WEBSITE:

USERNAME:

PASSWORD:

NOTES:

WEBSITE:

USERNAME:

PASSWORD:

NOTES:

WEBSITE:

USERNAME:

PASSWORD:

NOTES:

🌐WEBSITE:

👤USERNAME:

🔒 PASSWORD:

📋NOTES:

🌐WEBSITE:

👤USERNAME:

🔒 PASSWORD:

📋NOTES:

🌐WEBSITE:

👤USERNAME:

🔒 PASSWORD:

📋NOTES:

🌐WEBSITE:

👤USERNAME:

🔒 PASSWORD:

📋NOTES:

WEBSITE:

USERNAME:

PASSWORD:

NOTES:

WEBSITE:

USERNAME:

PASSWORD:

NOTES:

WEBSITE:

USERNAME:

PASSWORD:

NOTES:

WEBSITE:

USERNAME:

PASSWORD:

NOTES:

WEBSITE:

USERNAME:

PASSWORD:

NOTES:

WEBSITE:

USERNAME:

PASSWORD:

NOTES:

WEBSITE:

USERNAME:

PASSWORD:

NOTES:

WEBSITE:

USERNAME:

PASSWORD:

NOTES:

🌐 WEBSITE:

👤 USERNAME:

🔒 PASSWORD:

📋 NOTES:

🌐 WEBSITE:

👤 USERNAME:

🔒 PASSWORD:

📋 NOTES:

🌐 WEBSITE:

👤 USERNAME:

🔒 PASSWORD:

📋 NOTES:

🌐 WEBSITE:

👤 USERNAME:

🔒 PASSWORD:

📋 NOTES:

Z

🌐 WEBSITE:

👤 USERNAME:

🔒 PASSWORD:

📋 NOTES:

🌐 WEBSITE:

👤 USERNAME:

🔒 PASSWORD:

📋 NOTES:

🌐 WEBSITE:

👤 USERNAME:

🔒 PASSWORD:

📋 NOTES:

🌐 WEBSITE:

👤 USERNAME:

🔒 PASSWORD:

📋 NOTES:

Manufactured by Amazon.ca
Acheson, AB

10396733R00061